COLOR
CODING
YOUR
SCRIPTURES

A Quick and Easy Way
to Improve Your Scripture Study

SANDRA B. BLACK

Covenant Communications, Inc.

This book is dedicated to the One who inspired the code to give me a clearer understanding of his scriptures,

And to my family and friends who encouraged me to write about it.

ABOUT THE AUTHOR

An early morning seminary teacher for over eight years, Sandra Baton Black is a homemaker as well as a former temple organist. She enjoys teaching in all its facets and served a mission at the Missionary Training Center tutoring reading. She also loves flower arranging, quilting, and painting everything from the house to a variety of crafts.

The mother of twelve children, Sister Black makes her home in Orem, Utah.

Color-Coding Your Scriptures: A Quick and Easy Guide to Improving Your Scripture Study is her first publication.

Published by Covenant Communications, Inc.
American Fork, Utah

Printed in the United States of America
First Printing: February 2012

13 12   14 13 12 10

ISBN 13: 978-1-57734-191-8   ISBN 10: 1-57734-191-0

COLOR-CODING YOUR SCRIPTURES

A Quick and Easy Guide to Improving Your Scripture Study

I discovered color-coding during the almost nine years I taught early morning seminary. I attended a seminary faculty meeting and heard a veteran teacher describe how she had her students color their scriptures. This thought was intriguing to me. What could anyone learn by coloring the scriptures?

Curiosity finally got the best of me, so I asked about this teacher's purpose and method of coloring her scriptures. Her explanation was not in-depth, and so did not help me, but my curiosity would not let me give up. I believed that there had to be a way to mark my scriptures that would ease the pain of my learning disability. I had a faulty short-term memory; some refer to it as a lack of reading comprehension. I wanted to remember what I had read after I read it. I was intrigued by the idea that I could look at a page of scripture and know what was happening without having to read it all over again.

Consequently, I bought myself some colored pencils, did a lot of praying, and set out on a surprisingly grand adventure.

If you've ever read a verse or two of scripture, stopped and asked yourself, "What did I just read?" and not known the answer, you'll love coloring your scriptures. Likewise, if you've ever been asked by a teacher to read a verse and then explain it; or if you've ever hunted for a scripture you knew you'd read just recently, but couldn't find it; or if you teach from the scriptures and want to be able to pick out the most important parts of a chapter easily, you'll love having colored scriptures. If you want to be able to discern history from doctrine or genealogy from geography by just looking at the page, you'll love coloring your scriptures.

When you read a verse of scripture with color-coding in mind, it helps you to concentrate on what you're reading so that you can discern the correct color. Since this keeps you focused upon the content of the scripture, it keeps your mind from wandering, so you will more easily remember what you read. When you read with this kind of attention and focus, you are also better able to answer questions about what you read.

When you've color-coded all your scriptures (and you'll find the journey is even more fun than the destination), you'll be able to open to any page in your scriptures and see immediately if God or a prophet is speaking and if the page has genealogy or geographical information, parables or spiritual gifts, or a combination of these.

Coloring your scriptures takes very little time if you color only the verse number and not the entire verse. It's so easy and quick you can even do it during family scripture study with only a second's delay between verses. (I'll explain how later.) Coloring your scriptures will—

• help you learn more than you ever dreamed possible,
• motivate you to consult commentaries and other reliable sources for further understanding, and
• allow you to feast upon the scriptures, pondering them instead of just reading them.

2

In addition, as you use prayer with your study, the Spirit will guide you to a greater knowledge of the gospel of Jesus Christ.

Don't keep the color code to yourself. Children and teenagers also enjoy color-coding. As your little ones see you enjoying coloring your scriptures, they will ask you to teach them, too. (They are especially drawn to the colored pencils!) Many parents buy videos and tapes for their children, hoping that they will learn about the scriptures. How much better it is to have them actually engrossed in the scriptures themselves. What a fun family home evening you could have while teaching color-coding to your loved ones!

Anyone can buy and own a set of scriptures, but let us be wise stewards in using and applying them to their best advantage. As President Kimball said, "Do it!"

Tools You Will Need

To prepare for color-coding, you will need a set of nine colored pencils in the following colors: red, green, purple, blue, orange, yellow, brown, pink, and black. (You may choose your own colors according to what you have around the house if you wish; I've found these colors help me remember what they stand for. I'll explain why later.) I like pencils that have erasers on them, since I have some-times needed to erase mistakes, and sometimes I change my mind about which color is most appropriate.

You'll find that an erasable red ballpoint pen is handy for underlining and writing comments in the margins as well as for marking the words of Isaiah. Mistakes can be erased, and erasable pens don't bleed through the paper. Red ink shows up more clearly than red pencil, and pens don't have to be sharpened constantly, as pencils do.

You will also need a six-inch ruler for underlining words and phrases neatly. Clear plastic is best because you can see the print through it, and get your line just where you want it.

The hardest item of all to obtain will most likely be time to study. Don't be fooled into thinking that TV programs, housework, yardwork, avocations, recreational activities, or pastimes are more important than studying your scriptures. You've probably seen the object lesson where a Ping-Pong ball is placed in a pint jar, which is then filled with beans. Everything fits cozily. But if you pour everything out and put the beans in first, there isn't enough room left for the Ping-Pong ball.

That object lesson applies to scripture study as well as many other things that we are asked to do. If you let the Ping-Pong ball represent reading your scriptures and the beans represent all the chores and pastimes of life, you'll understand the moral. If you take time early in the morning to study your scriptures, there's time in the day for everything that's really important. If you wait and try to find time later, there will be none.

I have found an additional advantage when I study early in the morning: it's easier for me to hear the Spirit. While it is true that any quiet time you can find will be of value to you, it's easier for me to stay awake early in the morning than after the family has gone to bed.

Bruce R. McConkie said, "I think that people who study the scriptures get a dimension to their life that nobody else gets and that can't be gained in any way except by studying the scriptures. There's an increase in faith and a desire to do what's right and a feeling of inspiration and understanding that comes to people who study the gospel—meaning particularly the standard works—and who ponder the principles that can't come in any other way" (Bruce R. McConkie, *Church News,* 24 January 1976, p. 4).

You will also gain a greater feeling of charity for others, which, above all else, is required for entrance into the celestial kingdom. We are told in Moroni 10:21: "And except ye have charity ye can in nowise be saved in the kingdom of God. . . ."

Finally, remember the counsel found in Doctrine and Covenants 130:18-19: "Whatever principle of intelligence we attain unto in this life, it will rise with us in the resurrection. And if a person gains more knowledge and intelligence in this life through his diligence and obedience than another, he will have so much the advantage in the world to come."

I promise you that studying the scriptures releases in you new feelings of charity that you have not experienced before. Your diligence and obedience in studying the scriptures will not go unnoticed and will bring great blessings to you.

Let's Begin

The first rule to remember when studying the scriptures is that the more you study, the more you understand. For this reason, the color you choose for a particular verse today may not be the color you would choose next year. That's one of the reasons I suggest using colored pencils and not something more permanent. You can always change the color.

As you color your scriptures, you will see the organization of the chapter as you have never seen it before.

To color code your scriptures, simply draw a box around the verse number and color it in. Do not underline the entire verse with the color. The scriptures in this booklet have the box around the verse numbers so that you can practice the process.

It is best to start with one color at a time and learn where to use it before you go on to another color. Red is the easiest because it is usually the most obvious.

If you're the adventurous type, however, you might want to start at the beginning of any book of scripture, and using the color guide on the back cover of this book, begin reading and marking each scripture as you decide which color fits the verse.

Now, on to each of the color definitions. . . .

RED

Have you ever seen a red-letter edition of the Bible? All the words of God are printed in red ink, and everything else is printed in black ink. This makes the words of God stand out so they can be found very easily.

You can make your scriptures similar to the red-letter edition of the Bible simply by drawing a box or a circle around the verse *number* of any verse where God is speaking. You don't need to underline the entire verse. That just makes your scriptures messy and more difficult to read.

When you have identified a verse in which God is speaking (or any member of the Godhead), color the verse number with your red pencil. (The first verse has no number, so you may choose to do this with the first letter instead.) This doesn't take much time or energy, and it sets the words of God off from the rest of the page. At the same time, it keeps your pages neat and pleasing to the eye.

The gospels of the New Testament are a good place to begin because the words of Christ are abundant there. Matthew 3:15 is a good example:

15 And Jesus answering said unto him, Suffer it to be so now: for thus it becometh us to fulfil all righteousness. Then he suffered him.

Because Jesus is speaking, a box is drawn around the verse number and then colored red. However, when a verse says only that God "spoke" to an individual, you do not need to mark it in red. This is because it is not a direct quote.

The Lord speaks in the Old Testament, too. We read in Exodus 24:12:

12 And the Lord said unto Moses, Come up to me into the mount, and be there: and I will give thee tables of stone, and a law, and commandments which I have written; that thou mayest teach them.

God often sends angels to communicate with us. When a heavenly messanger brings a message from God, red should be used even though God himself is not speaking. For instance, in Luke 1:26-25, we read that the angel Gabriel is sent from God to Mary with this message:

35 And the angel answered and said unto her, The Holy Ghost shall come upon thee, and the power of the Highest shall overshadow thee: therefore also that holy thing which shall be born of thee shall be called the Son of God.

If a verse seems to require more than one color, red always predominates, because the words of the Godhead are more important than anything else we can learn. For instance, in Genesis 12:7 God appears, he speaks, and Abram builds an altar.

> [7] And the Lord appeared unto Abram, and said, Unto thy seed will I give this land: and there builded he an altar unto the Lord, who appeared unto him.

The verse could be colored orange for spiritual gifts or blue for story line, but ask yourself, "Which is more important?" Isn't God's promise more important than the fact that he appeared to Abram, and more important than the fact that Abram built an altar? So red is the best color to use here.

In the gospels of the New Testament, since much of what is there is obviously the Lord's counsel, I prefer to color the prophecies orange and make them stand out from the other counsel of the Lord. However, you do what makes the most sense to you.

In a conversation between the Lord and another person, the Lord's side of the conversation may be a very small part of the verse. In Genesis 18:28 Abraham is bargaining with the Lord on behalf of Sodom and Gomorrah, or more correctly, on behalf of Lot and his family:

> [28] "Peradventure there shall lack five of the fifty righteous: wilt thou destroy all the city for lack of five?

The Lord's short answer, "If I find there forty and five, I will not destroy it," is found at the end of the verse.

Which do you feel is most important, Abraham's question or the Lord's answer? Your answer will determine whether you color this verse red, green, or blue.

BLUE

Blue is used to show what people are doing or what is happening to the people in the story. Blue is the main color of the Book of Mormon, the Old Testament, and the Gospels of the New Testament, because they are about people. Blue identifies the story line and describes people's experiences. It answers the question, "What is happening?" Is someone speaking, asking a question, or just waiting for someone? Are they fighting a war, singing a song, or eating a meal?

Blue is used more than any other color, so if you can't decide which color to use, it could very well be blue. In Matthew 13:11 the Savior is speaking, so color the verse number red. The action that causes the Savior to speak is described in verse 10, just before it, so color the verse number blue.

10 And the disciples came, and said unto him, Why speakest thou unto them in parables?
11 He answered and said unto them, Because it is given unto you to know the mysteries of the kingdom of heaven, but to them it is not given.

Genesis 37:29-31 provides another good example:

29 And Reuben returned unto the pit; and, behold, Joseph was not in the pit; and he rent his clothes.
30 And he returned unto his brethren, and said, The child is not; and I, whither shall I go?

[31] And they took Joseph's coat, and killed a kid of the goats, and dipped the coat in the blood;

These last verses from the story of Joseph and his coat of many colors tell what Joseph's brothers were doing. Color the verse numbers blue.

Blue doesn't necessarily mean movement and action; it can show *doing* but also just *being*. For instance in 2 Chronicles 16:12 we read:

[12] And Asa in the thirty and ninth year of his reign was diseased in his feet, until his disease was exceeding great. . . .

Asa isn't *doing* anything; he is simply *being* sick. Disease is what is happening to him.

When ordinary people (not the Savior or the prophet) are speaking, color the scripture blue, as in John 7:20:

[20] The people answered and said, Thou hast a devil: who goeth about to kill thee?

Lists of people such as in Nehemiah 10:1-28 can be colored blue. These are the people who covenanted to keep the law of God. Ezra 10:18-44 lists the men who took strange (or foreign) wives, another action that can be colored blue.

PURPLE

Anything that would appear on a family group sheet or pedigree chart should be marked purple, the color of kings, whose ancestry is always kept. Whenever you read that a person is born, gets married, dies, or is buried, color the number of the verse purple. The "begats" are, of course, the most obvious verses to be colored purple. A good example is Matthew 1:1-16:

The book of the generation of Jesus Christ, the son of David, the son of Abraham.

2 Abraham begat Isaac; and Isaac begat Jacob; and Jacob begat Judas and his brethren, etc.

Sometimes the genealogical information is given as part of a story, and not in lists. See, for instance, Genesis 29:33:

33 And she conceived again, and bare a son; and said, Because the Lord hath heard that I was hated, he hath therefore given me this son also: and she called his name Simeon.

The scriptures are filled with births and deaths of people whose names are not mentioned. The verses can still be colored purple. 3 Nephi 2:11 reads:

And it came to pass in the thirteenth year there began to be wars and contentions throughout all the land; for the Gadianton robbers had become so numerous, and did slay so many of the people, and did lay waste so many cities, and did spread so much death and carnage throughout the land, that it became expedient that all the people, both the Nephites and the Lamanites, should take up arms against them.

Both 3 Nephi 2:9 and Alma 45:18 can also be colored purple:

[9] And Nephi, who was the father of Nephi, who had the charge of the records, did not return to the land of Zarahemla, and could nowhere be found in all the land.

[18] And when Alma had done this he departed out of the land of Zarahemla, as if to go into the land of Melek. And it came to pass that he was never heard of more; as to his death or burial we know not of.

The scriptures don't tell us that Nephi or Alma died, but they were never seen again so we assume they were translated or lifted up. Because their mortal lives are over, mark these verses purple.

ORANGE

Spiritual gifts are an important subject to highlight. These are certainly bright episodes in people's lives, so they are colored orange. Spiritual gifts include dreams, visions, prophecy, the gifts of tongues, healing the sick or raising the dead—anything that is done with, or by, the Spirit. Matthew 4:11 and 4:23 provide excellent examples:

[11] Then the devil leaveth him, and behold, angels came and ministered unto him.

[23] And Jesus went about all Galilee, teaching in their synagogues, and preaching the gospel of the kingdom, and healing all manner of sickness and all manner of disease among the people.

Another less obvious place for orange is when we read that the Lord spoke, although his words aren't given until the next verse. Having the Lord speak to you is certainly a spiritual gift. In Joshua 4:15-16 below, orange would be used to mark verse 15, to indicate the spiritual gift of communication with God. In verse 16, red would be used to show that the Lord is speaking:

15 And the Lord spake unto Joshua, saying,
16 Command the priests that bear the ark of the testimony, that they come up out of Jordan.

Good king Hezekiah received spiritual gifts, as described in 2 Kings 18:7:

7 And the Lord was with him; and he prospered whithersoever he went forth: and he rebelled against the king of Assyria, and served him not.

Certainly, Hezekiah received heavenly help. Color this verse number orange.

When the Lord gives you power to carry heavy burdens with ease, that is also a spiritual gift as in Mosiah 24:15:

15 And now it came to pass that the burdens which were laid upon Alma and his brethren were made light; yea, the Lord did strengthen them that they could bear up their burdens with ease, and they did submit cheerfully and with patience to all the will of the Lord.

In John 6:5-14 we read that Jesus took five barley loaves and two small fish and fed five thousand people. That in itself is a miracle and should be colored orange. But we read of yet another miracle in verse 13:

13 Therefore they gathered them together, and filled twelve baskets with the fragments of the five barley loaves, which remained over and above unto them that had eaten.

In Exodus chapter 16 we read that the children of Israel were given manna and quail to eat. Verse 35 below tells us that they ate for forty years without plowing, sowing, or reaping, another spiritual gift, so color the verse number orange.

35 And the children of Israel did eat manna forty years, until they came to a land inhabited; they did eat manna, until they came unto the borders of the land of Canaan.

Prophecy is a spiritual gift and we find a lot of it in the scriptures. 1 Nephi 12:12 tells of Columbus and his voyage long before he was born:

12 And I looked and beheld a man among the Gentiles, who was separated from the seed of my brethren by the many waters; and I beheld the Spirit of God, that it came down and wrought upon the man; and he went forth upon the many waters, even unto the seed of my brethren, who were in the promised land.

Sometimes prophecy is difficult to recognize because it hasn't come to pass yet. Or possibly you haven't understood what you read. The key is to watch for the word "shall" or "it shall come to pass." These words are often used in prophecy. Helaman 16:12 reads:

[12] Yea, I say unto you, that in the latter times the promises of the Lord have been extended to our brethren, the Lamanites; and notwithstanding the many afflictions which they <u>shall</u> have, and not withstanding they <u>shall</u> be driven to and fro upon the face of the earth, and be hunted, and <u>shall</u> be smitten and scattered abroad, having no place for refuge, the Lord <u>shall</u> be merciful unto them.

The prophecy is that the Lord shall be merciful, so it can be colored orange.

Some scriptures, such as Jacob 5, may be both an allegory and also a prophecy of things to come. You will have to choose whether to mark it as a prophecy/spiritual gift and color it orange, or as a parable and color it yellow.

GREEN

Green is used to mark prophets' words and teachings as well as any explanations. Green is an important color because it is the "living" part of the scriptures. The teachings of the prophets can be their own words or the words of God as quoted by them. You must decide if you only want to know when a prophet is speaking as a prophet, or if you want to mark everything he says in green.

In John 1:29, John the Baptist identifies Jesus Christ:

[29] The next day John seeth Jesus coming unto him, and saith, Behold the Lamb of God, which taketh away the sin of the world.

15

We read in the Bible Dictionary that "Jesus praised John as a prophet, saying there is none who was greater (Matt. 11:7-11)." So color the verse number green.

In addition to the words of the prophets, there are certain explanations and teachings in the scriptures you will want to mark with green. The Book of Mormon is filled with explanations that begin: "And thus we see . . ." such as 1 Nephi 17:3:

> [3] And thus we see that the commandments of God must be fulfilled. And if it so be that the children of men keep the commandments of God he doth nourish them, and strengthen them, and provide means whereby they can accomplish the thing which he has commanded them; wherefore he did provide means for us while we did sojourn in the wilderness.

An example of an explanation from the Bible is found in Matthew 26:56:

> [56] But all this was done, that the scriptures of the prophets might be fulfilled. Then all the disciples forsook him, and fled.

While the first sentence is an explanation, the second sentence describes the action of the disciples (they "fled"), so you may want to mark this verse blue.

Although Lehi was the prophet when Nephi was commanded to make plates on which to keep a record of his people, Nephi gives an explanation of why he kept the records, so his words are colored green in 1 Nephi 19:

> [A]nd it came to pass that the Lord commanded me, wherefore I did make plates of ore that I might engraven

16

upon them the record of my people. And upon the plates which I made I did engraven the record of my father, and also our journeyings in the wilderness, and the prophecies of my father; and also many of mine own prophecies have I engraven upon them. . . .

David was never a prophet, but he gives some wise counsel in the Psalms, as in Psalm 125:

They that trust in the Lord shall be as mount Zion, which cannot be removed, but abideth for ever.

You will want to mark some of the Psalms green for teaching and explanation or pink for praise.

YELLOW

The Lord and his prophets have often used parables to teach us. A parable "conveys to the hearer religious truth exactly in proportion to his faith and intelligence; to the dull and uninspired it is a mere story" (Bible Dictionary). A parable veils its meaning so that one who is not ready for spiritual truth is not held accountable for it. Many parables deal with planting and harvest, so yellow is a good color to use to mark these scriptures. Yellow reminds us that we need light to grow.

For example, we can find one parable dealing with harvest in Luke 8:5 as well as its interpretation in verse 11:

5 A sower went out to sow his seed: and as he sowed, some fell by the way side; and it was trodden down, and the fowls of the air devoured it.

11 Now the parable is this: the seed is the word of God.

17

Parables often use similes and metaphors, both of which express a resemblance between one thing and another. The parable of the pearl of great price in Matthew 13:45-46 begins with a comparison, or simile:

> 45 Again, the kingdom of heaven is like unto a merchant man, seeking goodly pearls:
> 46 Who, when he had found one pearl of great price, went and sold all that he had, and bought it.

To some, this might be a story about a merchant who bought a very valuable pearl; to others, it is a parable that teaches the value and price of eternal life. It depends upon the spiritual capacity of the listener.

Some parables include their interpretation, as does the parable of the tares in Matthew 13:24-30. Its interpretation follows in verses 37-43, given below:

> 37 He answered and said unto them, He that soweth the good seed is the Son of man;
> 38 The field is the world; the good seed are the children of the kingdom; but the tares are the children of the wicked one;
> 39 The enemy that sowed them is the devil; the harvest is the end of the world; and the reapers are the angels.

Not all parables and similes include interpretations, but they are colored yellow anyway. A good example is Luke 17:7-9:

> 7 But which of you, having a servant plowing or feeding cattle, will say unto him by and by, when he is come from the field, Go and sit down to meat?

18

[8] And will not rather say unto him, Make ready wherewith I may sup, and gird thyself, and serve me, till I have eaten and drunken; and afterward thou shalt eat and drink?

[9] Doth he thank that servant because he did the things that were commanded him? I trow not.

The Lord taught David the enormity of his sin with this parable in 2 Samuel 12:1-4

[A]nd the Lord sent Nathan unto David. And he came unto him, and said unto him, there were two men in one city, the one rich, and the other poor.

[2] The rich man had exceeding many flocks and herds:

[3] But the poor man had nothing, save one little ewe lamb, which he had bought and nourished up: and it grew up together with him, and with his children; it did eat of his own meat, and drank of his own cup, and lay in his bosom, and was unto him as a daughter.

[4] And there came a traveller unto the rich man, and he spared to take of his own flock and of his own herd to dress for the wayfaring man that was come unto him; but took the poor man's lamb, and dressed it for the man that was come to him.

David's reaction and the interpretation for the parable is found in 2 Samuel 12:5 and 7. Mark verse 5 blue because it tells what David is doing. Mark verse 7 yellow because Nathan interprets here his parable for David.

[5] And David's anger was greatly kindled against the man; and he said to Nathan, As the Lord liveth, the man that hath done this thing shall surely die:

[7] And Nathan said to David, Thou art the man. . . .

Comparisons are often very subtle, as in John 12:24 where Jesus uses a corn of wheat to teach the reason for his coming death:

> 24 Verily, verily, I say unto you, Except a corn of wheat fall into the ground and die, it abideth alone: but if it die, it bringeth forth much fruit.

Jesus is comparing his death and resurrection to the wheat, so mark this verse yellow.

Allegories are very similar to parables. An allegory uses a comparison to present an abstract or spiritual lesson. For example, the allegory of the tame and wild olive trees in Jacob 5 compares the House of Israel and the gentiles to olive trees in order to teach us about the scattering and gathering of Israel. The allegory begins with a comparison:

> 3 For behold, thus saith the Lord, I will liken thee, O house of Israel, like unto a tame olive-tree, which a man took and nourished in his vineyard; and it grew, and waxed old, and began to decay.

Because parables, similes, and allegories all involve some comparison between different things, you may sometimes find it difficult to distinguish between them. For the sake of simplicity, when you see that a spiritual truth is being taught by comparison to an object, mark the verse yellow.

BROWN

In order to keep track of where people are, where they move to, and what the country around them looks like, verses that denote travel or give geographical descriptions are colored brown, the color of the earth.

Captain Moroni's stratagem for defeating the Lamanites involves a geographical description. It is found in Alma 43:31-32:

> [31] Therefore, he divided his army and brought a part over into the valley, and concealed them on the east, and on the south of the hill Riplah;
> [32] And the remainder he concealed in the west valley, on the west of the river Sidon, and so down into the borders of the land Manti.

The description helps you visualize the battle between Moroni's forces and the Lamanites. Color it brown.

Exodus 12:37 provides another good example:

> [37] And the children of Israel journeyed from Rameses to Succoth, about six hundred thousand on foot that were men, beside children.

> [41] And it came to pass at the end of the four hundred and thirty years, even the selfsame day it came to pass, that all the hosts of the Lord went out from the land of Egypt.

This color helps one get an overview of the movement in the book of scripture being read. Knowing where people are sometimes helps you to understand why people do the things they do.

For example, in Judges 9:32 a king's brother flees, so color the verse number brown.

> [21] And Jotham ran away, and fled, and went to Beer, and dwelt there, for fear of Abimelech his brother.

When you are reading the scriptures, it is often helpful to look back to the last brown scripture verse to see where the Savior is preaching his sermon, the missionaries are preaching, or the armies are battling. For example, in Luke 4:16, Christ is preaching:

16 And he came to Nazareth, where he had been brought up: and, as his custom was, he went into the synagogue on the sabbath day, and stood up for to read.

Where did this important event happen? In Nazareth. How do you know? Because you colored it brown.

Genesis 3:24 tells us about an important trip from the garden of Eden to an earthly existence.

24 So he drove out the man; and he placed at the east of the garden of Eden Cherubims, and a flaming sword which turned every way, to keep the way of the tree of life.

Since it is important to know that Adam was no longer in the presence of God, draw a box around the verse number and color it brown.

Our understanding of the Book of Mormon and its peoples is also assisted by the description of the land in Alma 22:27:

27 And it came to pass that the king sent a proclamation throughout all the land, amongst all his people who were in all his land, who were in all the regions round about, which was bordering even to the sea, on the east and on the west, and which was divided from the land of Zarahemla by a narrow strip of wilderness, which ran

from the sea east even to the sea west, and round about on the borders of the seashore, and the borders of the wilderness which was on the north by the land of Zarahemla, through the borders of Manti, by the head of the river Sidon, running from the east towards the west— and thus were the Lamanites and the Nephites divided.

PINK

In the scriptures people are occasionally so overcome by the Spirit and so thankful for the blessings they've received, that they break out in praise to God. These verses are colored pink.

Included in the color pink are some of the psalms in the Old Testament and the Psalm of Nephi in the Book of Mormon, as well as individual verses of praise throughout the scriptures. A good example for pink is Mosiah 8:20:

[20] O how marvelous are the works of the Lord, and how long doth he suffer with his people; yea, and how blind and impenetrable are the understandings of the children of men; for they will not seek wisdom, neither do they desire that she should rule over them!

David wrote a song that is full of praise for the Lord that is found in 2 Samuel 22:2-51, which should be colored pink. Verses 2 and 3 are given below:

[2] And he said, The Lord is my rock, and my fortress, and my deliverer;
[3] The God of my rock; in him will I trust: he is my shield, and the horn of my salvation, my high tower, and my refuge, my saviour; thou savest me from violence.

In 1 Nephi 1:14 Nephi records his father's words of praise:

> 14 And it came to pass that when my father had read and seen many great and marvelous things, he did exclaim many things unto the Lord, such as: Great and marvelous are thy works, O Lord God Almighty! Thy throne is high in the heavens, and thy power, and goodness, and mercy are over all the inhabitants of the earth; and, because thou art merciful, thou wilt not suffer those who come unto thee that they shall perish!

Nephi was so impressed with his father's words that he included them in his record. He writes himself in 2 Nephi 9:19-20.

> 19 O the greatness of the mercy of our God, the Holy One of Israel! For he delivereth his saints from that awful monster the devil, and death, and hell, and that lake of fire and brimstone, which is endless torment.
> 20 O how great the holiness of our God! For he knoweth all things, and there is not anything save he knows it.

Notice the exclamation marks in these verses. They are indicative of jubilant speech, but not all words of praise are that strong. As you look at the Psalms, you will find that they are usually sweet words of praise, not jubilant words.

One last example is found in Exodus 18:10-11:

> 10 And Jethro said, Blessed be the Lord, who hath delivered you out of the hand of the Egyptians, and out

of the hand of Pharaoh, who hath delivered the people from under the hand of the Egyptians.

[11] Now I know that the Lord is greater than all gods: for in the thing wherein they dealt proudly he was above them.

When your faith becomes a little weak or you feel that God is not listening to you, read the scriptures you have colored pink. They will revive your faith and let you know that God not only hears your prayers, but in due time will answer them as well.

BLACK

The black deeds and sayings of Satan are colored black. You will find a few of these scriptures in Genesis in the Old Testament and in Moses in the Pearl of Great Price. You will want to mark his words of temptation to Christ in the New Testament, as well as the words of the legion of devils who chose to enter the bodies of swine. You may be surprised at how many black verses there are. Start with Genesis 3:1 and Moses 1:12:

[N]ow the serpent was more subtil than any beast of the field which the Lord God had made. And he said unto the woman, Yea, hath God said, Ye shall not eat of every tree of the garden?

[12] And it came to pass that when Moses had said these words, behold, Satan came tempting him, saying: Moses, son of man, worship me.

Notice that Genesis 3:1 has no verse number so the first letter of the scripture is colored.

25

In Luke 8:28 Jesus casts out a legion of devils:

[28] When he saw Jesus, he cried out, and fell down before him, and with a loud voice said, What have I to do with thee, Jesus, thou Son of God most high? I beseech thee, torment me not.

[29] (For he had commanded the unclean spirit to come out of the man. For oftentimes it had caught him: and he was kept bound with chains and in fetters; and he brake the bands, and was driven of the devil into the wilderness.)

Verse 29 doesn't contain Satan's words but it is about Satan and explains the preceding verse where Satan does speak.

Satan's words and deeds are also described in Alma 30:53 by Korihor, who is speaking with Alma:

[53] But behold, the devil hath deceived me; for he appeared unto me in the form of an angel, and said unto me: Go and reclaim this people, for they have all gone astray after an unknown God. And he said unto me: There is no God; yea, and he taught me that which I should say. And I have taught his words; and I taught them because they were pleasing unto the carnal mind; and I taught them, even until I had much success, insomuch that I verily believed that they were true; and for this cause I withstood the truth, even until I have brought this great curse upon me.

After relating the story of Korihor, Mormon concludes:

[60] And thus we see the end of him who perverteth the ways of the Lord; and thus we see that the devil will not

support his children at the last day, but doth speedily drag them down to hell.

The phrase "and thus we see" indicates that this is an explanation, which should be marked green. However, this verse also describes how we can expect Satan to act. You decide which color to use on this verse.

The most obvious color for anything related to Satan is black. The world often dresses Satan in black. The ugly things people do when under his influence are called "black deeds." Therefore, when Satan speaks in the scriptures, mark those verses black.

RED ERASABLE PEN

The Savior and Nephi both quoted Isaiah. You can set off Isaiah's verses by drawing a red box around the verse number with a red ballpoint pen. A good example is 2 Nephi 12:2:

2 And it shall come to pass in the last days, when the mountain of the Lord's house shall be established in the top of the mountains, and shall be exalted above the hills, and all nations shall flow unto it.

When we read Luke 4:18-19, we know that Jesus is quoting Isaiah because the first footnote for verse 18 refers the reader to Isaiah 61:1.

18 The Spirit of the Lord is upon me, because he hath anointed me to preach the gospel to the poor; he hath sent me to heal the brokenhearted, to preach deliverance to the captives, and recovering of sight to the blind, to set at liberty them that are bruised.

Draw a box with red ink around the verse numbers, and then circle the footnote letter as well. Whenever you mark a letter indicating a footnote, be sure to circle that letter at the bottom of the page to make it easier to find the next time you read these verses.

Color Coding the Doctrine and Covenants, the Gospels, and the Epistles

RED

Because the Doctrine and Covenants is comprised of revelations given to the Prophet Joseph Smith by God, most of the book would be colored red. This would be of little value, so by expanding the concept just a little, we can use red in this book of scripture to mark instead those scriptures that tell *about* God.

It is amazing how much is revealed about the Godhead if you're looking for it. For instance, D&C 1:11 tells us that he speaks to anyone who will listen:

11 Wherefore the voice of the Lord is unto the ends of the earth, that all that will hear may hear:

We learn from D&C 6:16 that God knows our thoughts and the intents of our hearts as no one else does:

16 Yea, I tell thee, that thou mayest know that there is none else save God that knowest thy thoughts and the intents of thy heart.

The Lord introduces himself in D&C 6:21:

21 Behold, I am Jesus Christ, the Son of God. I am the same that came unto mine own, and mine own received

me not. I am the light which shineth in darkness, and the darkness comprehendeth it not.

All of these verses tell us *about* the Lord, so draw a box around the verse number with your red pencil and color it in.

Sometimes in addition to giving other information, the verse tells us about the Savior. I like to color these verses red, too. I want to learn all I can about the Savior. For example, D&C 63:46 describes the work and also tells of the Lord's will at that time:

46 And now speedily visit the churches, expounding these things unto them, with my servant Oliver Cowdery. Behold, this is my will, obtaining moneys even as I have directed.

Likewise, in the New Testament, use red to mark anything that the apostles write *about God*. For example, 2 Peter 1:16 tells of the majesty of Jesus Christ:

16 For we have not followed cunningly devised fables, when we made known unto you the power and coming of our Lord Jesus Christ, but were eyewitnesses of his majesty.

One last example should suffice. In Jude 1:21 we learn, in counsel from Jude, that our Lord is merciful:

1 Keep yourselves in the love of God, looking for the mercy of our Lord Jesus Christ unto eternal life.

Because it is counsel, it can be colored green; however, since it also tells us about our Savior, I prefer to color it red. Red then is used for either the *words* of one of the Godhead or something *about* one of the Godhead.

BLUE

Blue is not as commonly used in the Doctrine and Covenants or the Epistles, because it is used to mark scriptures that tell what people are doing, and these scriptures are mostly doctrine. However, blue can still be used to describe what people are doing or what happens to them. Here is an example:

> [2]John Taylor and Willard Richards, two of the Twelve, were the only persons in the room at the time; the former was wounded in a savage manner with four balls, but has since recovered; the latter through the providence of God, escaped, without even a hole in his robe. (D&C 135:2)

D&C 7:2 is another example where blue could be used effectively:

> [5]After it was truly manifested unto this first elder that he had received a remission of his sins, he was entangled again in the vanities of the world;

Another example from the Epistles of the New Testament can be found in Hebrews 11:17:

> [17] By faith Abraham, when he was tried, offered up Isaac; and he that had received the promises offered up his only begotten son.

To summarize: Blue verses are about people, what they do, what they think, what they don't do. Blue verses are often action verses.

PURPLE

Purple is used in the same way in the Doctrine and Covenants and the Epistles as it is in the other scriptures. You might take purple one step further and color all verses purple that speak of God as our Father. See Hebrews 12:9:

> 9 Furthermore we have had fathers of our flesh which corrected us, and we gave them reverence: shall we not much rather be in subjection unto the Father of spirits, and live?

Because D&C 135:1 tells of the deaths of Joseph and Hyrum Smith, it could be colored either blue or purple:

> 1 To seal the testimony of this book and the Book of Mormon, we announce the martyrdom of Joseph Smith the Prophet, and Hyrum Smith the Patriarch. They were shot in Carthage jail, on the 27th of June, 1844, about five o'clock p.m., by an armed mob—painted black—of from 150 to 200 persons. Hyrum was shot first and fell calmly, exclaiming: I am a dead man! Joseph leaped from the window, and was shot dead in the attempt, exclaiming: O Lord my God! They were both shot after they were dead, in a brutal manner, and both received four balls.

GREEN

Since the Epistles of the New Testament are all the words of prophets, you might be tempted to color every verse in them green. However, this would not aid your study of the New Testament very much. By expanding the concept, you can use green to signify doctrine, direction, and counsel (which is given by prophets and apostles).

This makes green the main color of the Doctrine and Covenants and the Epistles of the New Testament because these are books of doctrine, direction, and counsel. For example, in D&C 67:11, we read:

> 11 For no man has seen God at any time in the flesh, except quickened by the Spirit of God.

This is an example of doctrine. An example of direction can be found in D&C 63:42:

> 42 Let my servant Newel K. Whitney retain his store, or in other words, the store, yet for a little season.

Color both of these verses green.

In the New Testament, the apostles' letters are filled with counsel. Open to any page and you'll likely find direction or counsel. The scripture below (1 Timothy 4:12) is a good example of counsel. It should be colored green.

> 12 Let no man despise thy youth; but be thou an example of the believers, in word, in conversation, in charity, in spirit, in faith, in purity.

ORANGE

Gifts of the Spirit are found in the New Testament as well as in the Doctrine and Covenants. The apostles wrote of spiritual gifts, and these verses can be colored orange, as with Philippians 4:7:

> 7 And the peace of God, which passeth all understanding, shall keep your hearts and minds through Christ Jesus.

What a wonderful gift! Another scripture from the Epistles that should be colored orange is found in 2 Peter 1:21:

21 For the prophecy came not in old time by the will of man: but holy men of God spake as they were moved by the Holy Ghost.

The Doctrine and Covenants also tells of many spiritual gifts. This book of scripture even begins with the gift of prophecy. In D&C 1:3 we learn what will happen when the voice of the Lord is sent unto all men:

3 And the rebellious shall be pierced with much sorrow; for their iniquities shall be spoken upon the housetops, and their secret acts shall be revealed.

Color it orange just as you would if it were in the Book of Mormon or the Gospels.

YELLOW

There are short references to familiar parables in the Doctrine and Covenants. These should be colored yellow. See D&C 38:26:

26 For what man among you having twelve sons, and is no respecter of them, and they serve him obediently, and he saith unto the one: Be thou clothed in robes and sit thou here; and to the other: Be thou clothed in rags and sit thou there—and looketh upon his sons and saith I am just?

The Apostle Paul uses the parable of the olive tree to teach the Christians of his day (and ours) to obey God's laws lest we receive the severity of God as ancient Israel did. See Romans 11:16-21:

16 For if the firstfruit be holy, the lump is also holy: and if the root be holy, so are the branches.

17 And if some of the branches be broken off, and thou, being a wild olive tree, wert graffed in among them, and with them partakest of the root and fatness of the olive tree;

18 Boast not against the branches. But if thou boast, thou bearest not the root, but the root thee. . . .

At times Paul uses a parable and gives the interpretation along with it, as he does in Ephesians 5:22-25:

23 For the husband is the head of the wife, even as Christ is the head of the church: and he is the saviour of the body. . . .

Color all these verses yellow.

BROWN

There are several verses in the Doctrine and Covenants that should be colored brown. For example, in Section 107:53 we read:

53 Three years previous to the death of Adam, he [Noah] called Seth, Enos, Cainan, Mahalaleel, Jared, Enoch, and Methuselah, who were all high priests, with the residue of his posterity who were righteous, into the valley of Adam-ondi-Ahman, and there bestowed upon them his last blessing.

This was a great meeting, and where it happened is important, so color it brown. Another brown verse in D&C 84:3 tells where the New Jerusalem will be built:

34

3 Which city shall be built, beginning at the temple lot, which is appointed by the finger of the Lord, in the western boundaries of the State of Missouri, and dedicated by the hand of Joseph Smith, Jun., and others with whom the Lord was well pleased.

Verse 4 continues the description and should also be colored brown. Where men are called on missions, you could also color these verses brown, as in D&C 52:7-10:

7 And again, verily I say unto you, let my servant Lyman Wight and my servant John Corrill take their journey speedily;
8 And also my servant John Murdock, and my servant Hyrum Smith, take their journey unto the same place by the way of Detroit. . . .

In the Epistles, the apostles tell to whom they are writing. Those verses should be colored brown. For instance, in 2 Corinthians 1:1 Paul writes:

1 Paul, an apostle of Jesus Christ by the will of God, and Timothy our brother, unto the church of God which is at Corinth.

When Paul speaks of his travels, these verses should also be colored brown.

PINK

At the dedication of the Kirtland temple, the Prophet Joseph said in the dedicatory prayer found in D&C 109:1:

1 Thanks be to thy name, O Lord God of Israel, who keepest covenant and showest mercy unto thy servants who walk uprightly before thee, with all their hearts—

This should be colored pink. Another verse that should be colored pink appears in Ephesians 1:3, where Paul expresses his thankfulness:

3 Blessed be the God and Father of our Lord Jesus Christ, who hath blessed us with all spiritual blessings in heavenly places in Christ.

Color it and any other expressions of thanksgiving pink.

BLACK

The Epistles of the New Testament and the Doctrine and Covenants give warnings about Satan that should be colored black. A warning to Joseph Smith about Satan's plans is found in D&C Section 10:

10 And, behold, Satan hath put it into their hearts to alter the words which you have caused to be written, or which you have translated, which have gone out of your hands. . . .

These verses reveal the wickedness of Satan. Color them black. We read about Satan's rebellion in the premortal world in D&C 29:36:

36 And it came to pass that Adam, being tempted of the devil—for, behold, the devil was before Adam, for he rebelled against me, saying, Give me thine honor, which is my power; and also a third part of the hosts of heaven turned he away from me because of their agency:

There is plenty of information in the scriptures about Satan to warn us of his plans and designs. Mark all of it black. New Testament writers also warned us of Satan's power, as in 1 John 2:22:

22 Who is a liar but he that denieth that Jesus is the Christ? He is antichrist, that denieth the Father and the Son.

Peter also warned of false teachers in 2 Peter 2:1:

1 But there were false prophets also among the people, even as there shall be false teachers among you who privily shall bring in damnable heresies, even denying the Lord that bought them, and bring upon themselves swift destruction.

SUMMARY

Now, that all sounds easy, doesn't it? But what if, after you've read a verse, you think it needs two colors? If one of the colors is red, because a member of the Godhead is speaking, use that color. Otherwise choose the color that will remind you what you wanted to remember about that verse.

Don't be afraid of coloring your scriptures "wrong." Color your scriptures according to your understanding at this moment. Later, after studying and learning more, you may see things differently and decide to change the color of a verse here or there. That's easy enough. Just erase it (being careful not to erase the printed number) and color it a new color.

It is my hope and prayer that you may enjoy the grand adventure that comes with coloring your scriptures, that you will enjoy your scripture study more, learn to see more in the scriptures than you ever have before, and that you feel closer to the Savior throughout the rest of your life.

COLOR KEY

RED: The words of any member of the Godhead

BLUE: The story line, chronology, action, movement; in other words, what is happening

PURPLE: The genealogy, the "begats," births, marriages, deaths, burials

ORANGE: Any spiritual gift (dreams, visions, prophecy, tongues, healing, the power to accomplish tasks, etc.)

GREEN: Teachings of prophets, any speech or explanation that you want to remember

YELLOW: Parables, allegories, similes

BROWN: Travel or geographical information

PINK: Words of praise to God

BLACK: The words and deeds of Satan

RED PEN: The words of Isaiah when quoted by others, footnotes, special passages